What Is the Trinity?

Jesus was weary
hungry
felt anger
in high demand
interrupted
experienced disappointment
friends let him down
betrayed

Basics of the Faith

Sean Michael Lucas, Series Editor

What Is the Trinity?

2012

David F. Wells

P&R
PUBLISHING
P.O. BOX 817 • PHILLIPSBURG • NEW JERSEY 08865-0817

Unless otherwise indicated, Scripture quotations are from *ESV Bible* ® (*The Holy Bible, English Standard Version* ®). Copyright © 2001 by Crossway Bibles, a publishing ministry of Good News Publishers. Used by permission. All rights reserved.

Italics within Scripture quotations indicate emphasis added.

ISBN: 978-1-59638-436-1 (pbk)
ISBN: 978-1-59638-556-6 (ePub)
ISBN: 978-1-59638-555-9 (Mobi)

Page design by Tobias Design

Printed in the United States of America

Library of Congress Cataloging-in-Publication Data

Wells, David F.
  What is the Trinity? / David F. Wells.
     p. cm. -- (Basics of the faith)
  Includes bibliographical references.
  ISBN 978-1-59638-436-1 (pbk.)
  1. Trinity. I. Title.
  BT111.3.W45 2012
  231'.044--dc23

                          2012012508

■ **This much is certain.** Had the Christian faith merely been a human invention, Christians would never have come up with the doctrine of the Trinity. This doctrine is too thorny to understand and too difficult to explain for anyone to have deliberately fabricated it. There is no other religion that has anything remotely like this. No, this is not the fruit of our imagination but a doctrine of the way things are. God is triune. Knowing him in his triunity is central to Christian faith. Indeed, without this truth, that faith is not Christian at all.

Given this doctrine's centrality, it may seem surprising that there is no single verse in the Bible, or even a single passage, that explains how it is that God can be one in being and yet have three centers of self-consciousness within his being: the Father, the Son, and the Holy Spirit. Why is this?

The teaching that God is triune has to be constructed from many passages for two main reasons. First, there are many facets to it. It is not a simple doctrine. Second, God's disclosure of himself did not take place all at once. He revealed his triune nature only gradually and across large stretches of time. It is therefore revealed across a large swath of Scripture.

God began by showing Israel that he is a single, unique being. Then he began to give intimations that he is also tripersonal. However, it was the incarnation in particular that made this conclusion inescapable, and it was Christ's resurrection and ascension that especially brought into focus the third member of the Godhead, the Holy Spirit. It is the Spirit's work to apply the redemption that Christ won on the cross. It was, then, in this redemptive process, initiated by God's grace, that the full nature of his triunity was revealed to us. "In a word," says B. B. Warfield, "Jesus Christ and the Holy Spirit are the fundamental proof of the Trinity."[1]

Early in the life of the church, God's triune nature was condensed into several brief creedal statements. Numerous heresies challenged the biblical teaching on God. This came to a head in the fourth century, and the church responded with the writing of the Nicene Creed in 325. This brilliant work quickly became a landmark in clarifying what the Scriptures teach and what we are to believe. This, and the other creeds which followed, were important because they gave the church a united voice in expressing what is true.

And yet, despite definitive statements like this, the doctrine of God's triunity has continued to be contested across the ages and down to our own time. Today the most vigorous assaults on the doctrine come from those who are most intent on building bridges to the other religions. Dispensing with the Father, Son, and Holy Spirit, as John Hick does,[2] undoubtedly opens the door to inter-religious dialog with Hindus, Buddhists, and Muslims. Unfortunately, those who walk this road from the Christian side have nothing left to bring to the table. At least, what they bring no longer has any footing in biblical revelation. It is no longer grounded in who God actually is. It is, therefore, no longer Christian.

What we need to do first is to see how God's own self-disclosure unfolded across time. Here we are thinking about *biblical teaching*. We begin with the truth that <u>God is one</u>. Following that, we will see how the distinctions between Father, Son, and Holy Spirit were established and developed. We then need, second, to think *historically* about how the early church helped us to understand these truths. We will conclude by thinking about some of the *practical* connections that flow from the biblical doctrine of the Trinity.

GOD IS ONE

It may seem odd to us today that God did not begin to make himself known by first demolishing the idea that there are other gods. After Abraham's descendants became a people, God instead began by teaching them that they had to be exclusively *loyal* to him. In the first of the Ten Commandments, we are told that we are to "have no other gods" before him (Ex. 20:3), which does not deny that there might be other gods. The second and third commandments do not attack polytheism either but simply shine a light on the glorious nature of Yahweh. Because representations of God inevitably misrepresent his greatness and so diminish him (Ex. 20:4), they are forbidden. Images and idols in the ancient world were typically made to symbolize a god or goddess so that the divine presence could become more real to worshippers. With respect to Yahweh, though, images always and inevitably misconstrue who he is. They make him less real, not more real. He becomes smaller, more manageable, and far less glorious. That is why these images are forbidden. In fact, the only image that ever did him justice, which truly portrayed who he is and what his character is like, was given to us in the incarnation. Christ was "the image of the invisible God" (Col. 1:15) and "the exact imprint of his nature" (Heb. 1:3). This is the reason Christ said, "Whoever has seen me has seen the Father" (John 14:9). Apart from the incarnation, there is no accurate, complete, true, and dependable representation of the being and character of God.

The Ten Commandments are put in the context of God's redemption of his people—"I am the LORD your God, who brought you out of the land of Egypt" (Ex. 20:2)—and this act of redemption demonstrated not only God's great power and extraordinary grace but also the emptiness of the Egyptians' paganism and the futility of their superstitions. The exodus showed that their gods were nonentities. However, it was not only the gods who were defeated, but also the whole pagan way of thinking about life that was upended.

Pagan gods and goddesses did not communicate. They gave no revelation of themselves. But pagans were always fearful of their actions. These divinities acted in life, and often those actions were destructive. The gods were unpredictable, sometimes bad tempered, and often pernicious. That is why they had to be placated by offerings. And the only way to discern what was happening was to do so intuitively. This intuition was coupled to a pantheistic view of life, in which the natural order and these supposed deities were linked together and moved in rhythm with each other. Acts in the natural realm had a payoff in the supernatural. It was thus possible to affect what the gods did by sacrifices and other forms of homage.

That there is this link between the natural and the supernatural is simply false. We know from Genesis 1:1 that there was no creation before "the beginning." Creation is not coeternal with God. Before the beginning of the created world, God dwelled alone. The universe was made by him, is providentially sustained by him, and is utterly dependent on him. However, God is not in any way dependent on this created universe, nor is his being to be confused with created reality (Acts 17:24–25), nor can we act on him or coerce from him what we want by our actions. He is completely independent of his creation.

That is the biblical starting point. And this is the context in which we must read the Ten Commandments, as well as the laws that follow after them. Moses declared that the greatest commandment is that "our God, the LORD is one," and we are to love him with all of our heart (Deut. 6:4–5). We cannot have any allegiance to any other god or ultimate concern but must be subject solely to the God by whom we have been created and then redeemed. This call to loyalty is also a call to understand ourselves within the biblical framework of creation. The call to exclusive loyalty rests on the truth that there is only one God and that God himself is one (see also Deut. 32:31–43; Pss. 83:18; 86:10).

This call to loyalty was, of course, immediately tested. We know from the very earliest history that God's people often yielded to the allure of other gods. God's people blended into their religious environment. They wanted the benefits that other gods supposedly could bring, and they did not trust God enough to be delivered from their fears of what those supernatural beings might do to them. Terrible consequences followed, not from the pagan gods themselves but from Yahweh, because of this unfaithfulness.

The prophets had the task of declaring what the consequences of disobedience would be. They demanded that *monotheism* be believed and polytheism be rejected. Isaiah, for example, recorded God as saying, "Before me no god was formed, nor shall there be any after me" (Isa. 43:10). Again, "I am the first and I am the last; besides me there is no god"

(Isa. 44:6; see also 45:21; 46:9); "I am the LORD, and there is no other" (Isa. 45:6). "From of old . . . no eye has seen a God besides you," Isaiah declared (Isa. 64:4). That being so, God had to be at the center of Israel's life and vision; otherwise, the Israelites would find that they had foolishly chased illusions to their own undoing.

Nothing in this picture changes when we come to the New Testament. Paul, reflecting this line of Old Testament teaching, confirmed the Corinthians' belief that the gods behind the idols have no reality at all and that "there is no God but one" (1 Cor. 8:4; cf. Ps. 115:4–8). This is what he taught everywhere. There is "one Lord" and "one God and Father of all" (Eph. 4:5–6). Actually, even the demons know that "God is one" (James 2:19; cf. 4:12). Their theological knowledge at this point is quite accurate. Their problem is that they have rebelled against what they know to be true (cf. Matt. 4:10).

All of this may seem like old hat to us. Today, we who live in the West are not being seduced by exotic deities, and the belief in monotheism is well established in our cultures. Overwhelming majorities in all Western societies say that they believe in God. At least, they think that he exists.

And yet, there is a key point of continuity with this ancient world that we need to see. It is that we too are tempted to construct our own spiritualities, based on our own intuitions about the meaning of life. Indeed, this is one of the more remarkable developments in the West since the 1960s. Alongside our undoubted secularism has arisen a remarkable, resurgent, and unexpected cultural spirituality. It is remarkable because it has sprouted up in societies that have long been in a secularizing mode, imagining that the only reality we need to consider is the one that we see, touch, taste, and experience. However, despite this outlook, there has emerged a spirituality that yearns for something more, for something other, for a greater dimension to life. It wants to have a skylight through which to see vertically and not simply a window through which to look out horizontally on the world. In both the US and, remarkably, Europe, eight out of ten people now say that they are spiritual. This, of course, includes those who are also religious, such as churchgoers. However, many who are "spiritual" are not religious. Indeed, they are hostile to all forms of organized religion.

Their spiritual yearning is now taking many different forms, such as the (sanitized) Hinduism of the New Age movement, kabbalah, radical environmentalism, and many self-made spiritualities. What they all have in common, though, is a view of reality that is pantheistic. All of them, in one way or another, assume that nature encloses and contains the sacred. And it assumes that the way we make contact with God is to find him in ourselves. He is there within our deepest self. That is why psychology now plays such a prominent role in so many of these spiritualities.

However, to declare one's belief in the Christian God is, at one and the same time, to reject this cultural spirituality *in toto*. God is indeed one in his being, but he is not one with nature. He indeed upholds the entire universe, is everywhere, and pervades every corner of life. Nevertheless, there is an invisible boundary between him and us, both with respect to his being and with respect to what we know. We cannot cross that boundary to know him savingly. He is not found in our deepest self. He is outside the range of our intuitive radar. In fact, we are alienated from him and shut out from his fellowship and knowledge. We cannot access him on our own terms and on our own timetable.

No, it is he who must cross that boundary if we are to know him. The initiative must be his, and the timing is his.

And this he has done in Christ. The Christian faith has to be the enemy of all natural spirituality, because Christianity must be true to its own self, true to the God who is there, and true to what reality really is like. And it must express itself in a Trinitarian form. It is not enough that we believe in God, as do these spiritualities, however vaguely. We must believe in one God who, in his being, is not confused with creation and who is also tripersonal—Father, Son, and Holy Spirit.

However, this truth, that God is tripersonal, came slowly. God did not disclose it all at once. There were intimations of it from the very beginning of his self-revelation, but it did not come into full bloom from our perspective until the incarnation and the resurrection.

GOD IS TRIPERSONAL

For centuries, rabbis were perplexed by some Old Testament passages that seem to point to multiple persons in the Godhead. For example, what are we to make of the plural pronouns in the early chapters of Genesis? In the creation account, there is the statement, "Let us make man in our image, after our likeness" (Gen. 1:26). God says about Adam, "The man has become like one of us in knowing good and evil" (Gen. 3:22). Still later, at Babel, God says, "Let us go down and there confuse their language" (Gen. 11:7). What are we to make of the word "us" in these passages? What are we to make of the three supernatural beings who visit Abraham a little later (Gen. 18:1–21) and whom he worships (Gen. 18:2–3)? And, perhaps most importantly, what are we to make of the many appearances in the Old Testament of the angel of the Lord, who, in some passages, it is quite clear, is divine and yet also distinct from Yahweh (e.g., Ex. 14:19–22; Judg. 6:11–24)?

In the exegesis of the early centuries and later, in the Reformation period, it was typical to see in these passages preincarnate appearances of Christ. There is something to be said for this view. Christ himself declared that one of the most stringent assertions of Isaiah was made because the prophet saw Christ's "glory and spoke of him" (John 12:41). If Isaiah saw Christ's glory long before the time of the incarnation, Christ might well have manifested himself in a nonincarnate way in the person of the angel of the Lord. And yet, without the full light of the incarnation shining back onto the Old Testament revelation, it is difficult to see in it a full doctrine of the Trinity. It was the incarnation that made inescapable what had, of course, been there from all eternity but was only hinted at in the earlier biblical record: God is one in being but also tripersonal.

Christ

Our focus here is not on Christ's humanity. It is a given that his conception was miraculous (Luke 1:35), but that he is like us in every other way, except for sin (Heb. 4:15; 1 Peter 1:19). He has to be. He had to share our humanity in its every aspect if he was to redeem it from the sin that had invaded it. Thus we read that he is a descendant of Abraham (Gal. 3:16) and of David (Rom. 1:3), and was born of a woman (Gal. 4:4). However, it is the way in which he brought the Trinity into focus as God's incarnate Son that we must concentrate on here.[3]

[margin note: Virgin meant young maiden]

What immediately strikes us when we read the Synoptic Gospels—Matthew, Mark, and Luke—is Christ's announcement that it was in and with him that the kingdom of God had dawned. What he was speaking of is the rule of God. This rule was not political. Rather, as a result of its inauguration, God's character and greatness were being unveiled, the evidence of which was that sin and its consequences were about to be overcome. This kingdom, of course, could not be decisively enacted without the cross, and it will not be consummated until Christ's return at the end of time.

What is striking about this is that even though we can seek the kingdom of God (Luke 12:31), it is only *God's* to give or to take away (Luke 12:32; Matt. 21:43). We can inherit it, pray for it, and enter it, but it is his *alone* to give. Only he can establish it. And that was happening in Jesus. This was the open signal that the Messiah had, indeed, come. God was now in human form. The prophets had seen the vision of God scattering his enemies (Mic. 4:11–13; Isa. 13:19), but now it was the ultimate enemy behind those enemies who was about to be vanquished. Only God could overcome such a great and mighty enemy. "But if it is by the Spirit of God that I cast out demons, then the kingdom of God has come upon you" (Matt. 12:28). Jesus was about to plunder the strong man's house, and that he did on the cross (Matt. 12:29; Col. 2:15), thereby bringing release from captivity and redemption from sin to his people.

The Synoptic Gospels show the *process* by which Christ was revealed as God incarnate, the one through whom the reign of God was being established. But his identity was unfolded in steps. It is no surprise, then, that in these gospels his divinity is more implicit in what he does than explicit in what he says. There are, though, some exceptions. These are mainly in the titles of Christ, like Son of Man, and in two passages in particular, Matthew 11:25–27 and Matthew 21:33–34. In these passages, he unequivocally asserts that he is uniquely divine. In the former, he says that he has a unique knowledge of the Father, one that only the Son has, and he says that all things have been placed in his hand. Did this happen before time began? That is the clear implication. And to this unique knowledge is added a unique redemptive mission.

However, most of what we have in these gospels is more veiled and indirect. Christ's identity can be read from the events of his life. Had he not been fully divine, for example, he could not have exercised authority over Satan (Matt. 4:1–11), nature (Matt. 8:23–27), disease (Matt. 9:1–8), and death (Matt. 9:18–16) as he did.

In John, however, the veil that is present in the Synoptic Gospels is stripped away. John's purpose in writing the gospel was not to speak of the process by which Christ's identity was made known but to point unambiguously to what that identity was. The gospel was written, he said, "so that you may believe that Jesus is the Christ, the Son of God" (John 20:31). This gospel is organized around Jesus' seven "I am" statements (John 6:35; 8:12; 10:9; 10:11; 11:25; 14:6; 15:1), which connect with God's great declaration of his name to Moses: "I AM WHO I AM" (Ex. 3:14; cf. John 8:58). However, it is the conceptual framing of this truth that we need to note here.

In his gospel, John says repeatedly that this divine Christ was "sent" into this world. He was sent from "above," sent from glory, sent into the world to become "flesh" and to dwell among us (John 1:14). It was, Jesus said, the Father who had sent him (John 5:23). "I have come down from heaven," he said, "not to do my own will but the will of him who sent me" (John 6:38). His word was not his alone, but "the Father's who sent me" (John 14:24). Was this merely the sending of a prophet, as God had done so many times before? No, it was not. Christ came from "above." "You," Christ said, "are from below; I am from above. You are of this world; I am not of this world" (John 8:23; cf. 8:42). It was from this other world, this world of God's glory (John 17:5), of God's very being, that he had been sent and had come.

Christ had not merely come from the presence of God; his eternal place was within the Godhead. He had been there for all eternity (John 17:5). "I came," he said, "from [out of] God" (John 8:42), and it was to God the Father that he was returning (John 16:28). It is here that the rudiments of the doctrine of the Trinity are becoming clear. This eternal God is one. However, Jesus said, "I and the Father are one" *could that 1 in spirit* (John 10:30), which was an unmistakable assertion that he was this one God. That is what his Jewish hearers rightly understood. And yet, Father and Son are distinct from each other. The Father sends; the Son comes.

Because of our familiarity with the incarnation, which is annually celebrated with cheer and gift giving, we some-times lose sight of its gravity. We joyfully remember it as the supreme expression of God's grace. And so it is. "For you know the grace of our Lord Jesus Christ, that though he was rich, yet for your sake he became poor, so that you by his poverty might become rich" (2 Cor. 8:9). But this event was itself an act of grace because of our extreme predicament. Christ came to do for us what we could not do for ourselves. And the problem is not only that we lack the virtue to com-mend ourselves to God, to win his approval, but also that we are up against powers of darkness that are immensely greater than we are. Against such mighty powers, Luther said, another and a greater power had to be revealed and had to act on our behalf, so that our bond to that darkness could be severed. Only Christ, the God-man, fully human and fully divine, could so identify with us in our own humanity, be so identified with our sin, that he could atone for it and then, by his infinite divine power, conquer all the supernatural evil into whose world that sin had led. What seemed like an earthly defeat on the cross, as Christ's life was snuffed out in ignominy, turned out to be a mighty spiritual victory.

The bells of celebration will peal for all eternity. The Son was sent, he came, he was incarnate, he conquered, and now he rules over all life (Eph. 1:21–22; Phil. 3:21; Acts 10:36).

Father

Nowhere does Jesus suggest, or the New Testament teach, that God is the Father of all in a redemptive sense, as the liberal Protestants once asserted and many still believe. He is not. He is only Father to those who are in Christ, and, as Christ said, many people are on the broad way that leads to destruction and only a few are on the narrow road that leads to life (Matt. 7:13–14).[4] God is known to us as Father only in and through Christ, and not everyone is in Christ.

We should not be surprised, therefore, that in the Old Testament God is rarely referred to as Father. The people of Israel are occasionally spoken of as being his "son" in the context of speaking of him as "father" (Deut. 32:6; Jer. 31:9; Mal. 2:10), as is the king (e.g., 2 Sam. 7:14). And there are a few comparisons between God and an earthly father: "As a father shows compassion to his children, so the LORD shows compassion to those who fear him" (Ps. 103:13; cf. Deut. 1:31). But it is not until the coming of Christ that the full picture of God's Trinitarian being becomes clear, in which there is the Father, the Son, and the Holy Spirit. God the Father awaited the fullness of time before he "sent forth his Son" into the world, and then he "sent the Spirit of his Son into our hearts, crying, 'Abba! Father!'" (Gal. 4:4, 6). It is in this light that we look back and see what we could never otherwise have seen clearly in the Old Testament.

How well we know God as our Father is a test of how well we have understood our faith and how well we know the purpose of Christ's coming. "For everything that Christ taught, everything that makes the New Testament new, and better than the Old, everything that is distinctively Christian as opposed to merely Jewish," J. I. Packer has said, "is summed up in the knowledge of the Fatherhood of God. 'Father' is the Christian name for God."5

While God is our Father, nowhere in the Bible is he ever called our Mother. It is true that there are several instances where he is, or may be, likened to a mother, or specifically to a mother bird. God is "*like* an eagle that stirs up its nest" (Deut. 32:11). Or, "*like* birds hovering, so the LORD of hosts will protect Jerusalem" (Isa. 31:5). God says that he is "*like* a woman in labor" who cries out (Isa. 42:14) over his people. "Can a mother forget her nursing child?" God asks rhetorically (Isa. 49:15). The implied answer is no. He can no more forget his people than can a mother her child. "As one whom his mother comforts," he says, "so I will comfort you" (Isa. 66:13). Finally, Jesus said to Jerusalem, "How often would I have gathered your children together *as* a hen gathers her chicks" (Matt. 23:37). In these and a few other texts, a parallel is established between God and a mother. It is done through similes. God is *like* a mother. Nowhere, though, is he said to *be* our Mother (any more than he is said to be a bird). On the other hand, he is said to *be* our Father. He is not just *like* a father. He *is* our heavenly Father. This is a metaphor that expresses a direct identity and not merely a similarity. The New Testament authors never say that Jesus is *like* a lamb of God or that he is *like* a redeemer. Rather, he *is* the Lamb of God, and he *is* our Redeemer. And in the same way, they never say that God is merely *like* a father. Repeatedly they say that he *is* our heavenly Father. And this is how Jesus taught us to approach him in prayer: "our Father in heaven" (Matt. 6:9).6

It is entirely inappropriate, then, to reconfigure the nature of God by making him both Father and Mother, as some have done in order to address contemporary gender issues. And it is also highly inappropriate to speak of the biblical Trinity of Father, Son, and Holy Spirit in alternative ways, such as Creator, Liberator, and Comforter, in order to circumvent the masculine language of Father and Son.

This truth about God as our Father is where his self-revelation has come into full bloom. There is nothing greater that can be known, nothing greater that can be said than this, that God is our Father and we are his children. "See what kind of love the Father has given us, that we should be called children of God; and so we are," exclaims John (1 John 3:1). Indeed, we are not only his children but also his "sons." Both men and women alike are his "sons." And the point of this is that, in the inheritance laws of that day, it was the sons to whom the property and wealth went. Paul, who uses the language of sonship often, draws the conclusion for us. If the Spirit of God dwells in us, we have been adopted as "sons"; if adopted, then the Spirit leads us to cry out, "Abba! Father!" And so it is that we know we are "heirs of God and fellow heirs with Christ" (Rom. 8:14–17). It is Paul's way of telling us that we have been given all the riches of our great heavenly Father through Christ, that there are no greater blessings that anyone could receive than what we have been given in Christ.

There is no question that there are many whose experience of their fathers has been far from ideal. Many carry wounds all of their lives as a result. And yet, the fact that we are aware of this damage itself tells us that we have an idea in our minds of what a good father is like. That is what has produced such disappointment in some people. Their fathers have fallen so far short of the ideal.

However, bad experiences with earthly fathers provide no reason to turn away from the thought of God as our heavenly Father, as some have done. The truth is actually the reverse. We can be grateful that, despite many disappointments with earthly fathers, we have a heavenly Father who will never wound us, never disappoint us, never forget us, and never abandon us, and who will always love us in Christ—even in our darkest moments, even when others have turned away from us.

Holy Spirit

The Holy Spirit has been called the "forgotten" member of the Trinity. Who, one wonders, has forgotten him? Certainly not anyone who has been reading Scripture regularly. From beginning to end, his presence and work are very evident. However, what we are told about the Holy Spirit unfolds as we move from the Old Testament into the New.[7]

In the Old Testament, the lens is wider; in the New Testament, it is narrower. In the Old, the Spirit of God is seen to be at work cosmically in creation, nature, and history (e.g., Gen. 1:2; Ps. 104:29–30; Isa. 40:7), as well as more personally. In the New, an important change takes place. Now the work of the Spirit and that of the Son are correlated in a way that was not possible prior to Christ's coming. Now it is the Spirit's work to point men and women to the incarnate and risen Christ. The Holy Spirit does this by illuminating their minds to understand the truth about Christ in Scripture, bringing conviction, opening their hearts to believe the gospel, giving faith that Christ might be believed, and applying Christ's saving work to them. With this focus in the New Testament, the cosmic dimension of what the Holy Spirit does fades from view. He is still active in all creation, but his connection with Christ occupies the attention of the New Testament. Indeed, the Spirit and the Son are even joined linguistically, which of course could not be the case in the Old Testament. He who is and always has been "the Spirit of God" (Rom. 8:14) is now also "the Spirit of Christ" (Rom. 8:9), "the Spirit of his Son" (Gal. 4:6), and "the Spirit of Jesus Christ" (Phil. 1:19).

Two truths now become clear. First, the Holy Spirit is divine in the same sense that the Father and the Son are divine. Second, the Holy Spirit is both personal and personally distinct from the Father and the Son.

If the Holy Spirit were not fully divine, and divine in the same sense in which the Father and Son are, how could the New Testament correlate them as it does? We are instructed, for example, to baptize "in the name of the Father and of the Son and of the Holy Spirit" (Matt. 28:19). And Paul concludes his second epistle to the Corinthians with the words, "The grace of the Lord Jesus Christ and the love of God and the fellowship of the Holy Spirit be with you all" (2 Cor. 13:14). The reason for this correlation is that the Holy Spirit shares the same divine essence as the Father and the Son. This is evident in the many ways in which each member of the Trinity is said to have the same divine attributes. The Father is eternal (Ps. 90:2), as is the Son (John 1:2), but so is the Holy Spirit (Heb. 9:14). The Father is holy (Rev. 15:4), as is the Son (Acts 3:14), and so is the Holy Spirit, for why else would Scripture call him "Holy"? The Father is glorious (Eph. 1:17), Christ is "the Lord of glory" (1 Cor. 2:8), and the Holy Spirit is "the Spirit of glory" (1 Peter 4:14). The Father is true (John 7:28), the Son is the personal embodiment of that truth (John 14:6), and it is also true that "the Spirit is the truth" (1 John 5:6). We should not be at all surprised to read that when Peter confronted Ananias, he first said that Ananias had lied "to the Holy Spirit" (Acts 5:3). Then he added: "You have not lied to men but to *God*" (Acts 5:4).

The Holy Spirit, then, is not simply an impersonal force or merely a synonym for God in action. He is a person who thinks, wills, and acts. It is the Holy Spirit, Jesus said to the apostles, who will "teach you all things" (John 14:26). He will "bear witness" to Christ (John 15:26; cf. Rom. 8:16; Heb. 10:15). He will "convict the world" of sin (John 16:8). He who spoke (Acts 8:29; 13:2; 16:6–7; 21:11) and gave utterance (Acts 2:4) now helps us (Rom. 8:26) and intercedes for us (Rom. 8:27). Here it is: teaching, speaking, giving utterance, bearing witness, convicting, leading, and praying. What else can we conclude but that these are the actions of a person? Indeed, they are the actions of the third person of the Godhead, the Holy Spirit.

The Holy Spirit was involved in Christ's incarnate life at its three most important points: the incarnation, the atonement, and the resurrection. First, it was the Holy Spirit who overshadowed Mary (Luke 1:35) to produce in her, by supernatural agency, that sinless humanity to which the eternal Word could be joined. Christ, therefore, was not simply a human teacher, no matter how great, a mere guru with compelling insights about life, but a unique breakthrough. He was one of a kind. He was as different from all other religious teachers as God is different from us. He was not great as we say some are; he was and is incomparable. And if the Father sent the Son, and if the Son thus became "God with us" (Matt. 1:23) through the incarnation, then it was by the agency of the Spirit that this mission was accomplished.

Second, it was "through the eternal Spirit" that Christ "offered himself without blemish to God" (Heb. 9:14). Christ laid aside the use of some of his divine prerogatives during his earthly life (cf. Phil. 2:5–12), but the Holy Spirit led him, sustained him against the attacks of Satan, and brought him to the point of his self-substitution on the cross successfully. What he did there, he did finally and conclusively. What he did there cannot be replicated and need never be repeated. It stands for all time and eternity.

Third, it was "according to the Spirit of holiness" that Christ "was declared to be the Son of God in power . . . by his resurrection from the dead" (Rom. 1:3–4). The resurrection was the public announcement made by God the Father, and effected by the Spirit, that Christ was God and that he had been triumphant. It announced the completion of his work and the defeat of all our spiritual enemies. Christ entered into a new expression of his sovereignty in which he rules, not merely by supreme divine power, but also on account of his defeat of evil at the cross. So it is that he is now the head of the church (Eph. 1:20–23; 1 Peter 3:21–22).

God's triunity is now taking unmistakable shape. Within this one being, there is a Father who is personally distinct from the Son and a Son who is distinct from the Holy Spirit. The Son speaks to the Father, who is other than himself: "Holy Father, keep them in your name" (John 17:11). The Father speaks to the Son. The Father "sent" him, and Christ's works were those "that the Father has given me to accomplish" (John 5:36). And, as we have just seen, the Holy Spirit was intimately involved in all phases of Christ's incarnate life and now points sinners to the second person of the Godhead, Christ, in whom alone salvation can be found. And this same Holy Spirit is "sent" into our hearts to witness to our spirits.

Although there must be much about life within the Godhead that we do not know, there are two facets that we especially need to note here. They are that, from all eternity, within the Godhead, there was love and communication.

Christ spoke of this love (John 17:26). As we have seen, there was much communication within the Godhead, as a result of which the Son and the Spirit were "sent" on their missions. It is important to reflect on this because we know only too well that in this fallen world, among the many deficiencies that we experience are the fracturing of love and the breakdown of communication. We long for real love and genuine communication in the midst of a world of harshness and broken relations. It is hard to find. Indeed, the Holy Spirit's work of sanctification is, in part, to restore the lost capacity for Christlike love and the lost ability to communicate in the fullness of God's holiness. And we do get small glimpses of what life could be like if it were lived solely in love and if communications were utterly truthful, open, and kind. We do begin to experience partially what our full restoration in these ways will be like. We have, though, only the down payment, and we long for what is to come when God's redemptive work within us reaches its culmination. It is to this future, exhibited from all eternity in the Trinity, that we are now journeying.

Second, the deep interconnection between the Son and the Spirit, which we have seen, also has an important practical consequence. It gives us a way to test claims in the church. We often hear people telling us about what God has been doing inside or outside the church or what he has been saying to people personally. In relation to these claims, here is a simple test: as a result of what God "has been doing," are we seeing Christ elevated? Are the truths about him taking root? Are eyes being opened, is worship following, and is repentance from sin happening?

If the Spirit was the agent in carrying out the will of the Father in Christ's incarnation and death, and if the work of the Spirit is now correlated with the work of the Son, then we cannot claim that the Spirit has been at work if Christ and his work have not been magnified. If the life, death, and resurrection of Christ are not being made central, if our eyes are not being drawn to him, if we are not seeing that sin must be forsaken and he must be fully trusted, then the

Holy Spirit has not been at work. Where men and women turn from themselves as their life's center and turn to Christ in trust, there we can say with confidence that God has been at work.

There is, then, one divine being, but within this one being there are three centers of self-consciousness: the Father, the Son, and the Holy Spirit. A person, Charles Hodge said in an earlier generation, "is an intelligent subject who can say I, who can be addressed as Thou, who can act and be the object of action."[8] That, indeed, is what we see in the Trinity in the communication among Father, Son, and Holy Spirit—all within the one being of God.

This is a profound mystery, but it is also a profound truth. It might be tempting to think that because we have difficulty in understanding how this can be, we can set it aside as being beyond us and, perhaps, irrelevant to Christian faith. That would be a great mistake. The gospel is simple only in the sense that the simplest people can understand enough of it to find acceptance with the Father through the work of the Son because of the working of the Spirit. But the gospel is not simplistic. We have sometimes made it so, but it is never other than the most profound truth that any person will ever encounter in life. It is a truth that brings our sin into the very depths of the being of God, face to face with his holiness, and it therefore brings us face to face with the infinite God. If the gospel is so simple that the simplest can understand it, it is also so profound that none can fully plumb its depths. We cannot sacrifice this profundity in the name of the gospel's simplicity, for then we will drift into superficiality. At the same time, in the name of the gospel's profundity, we cannot lose its simplicity; otherwise, it will not be a message for all people, and we will drift into irrelevance.

THE TRINITY DEFINED

Long before the New Testament canon was closed, there was heresy in the church. Indeed, Paul spoke of it. He had to confront it. And he saw days coming when the church would have to be defended against it. In his farewell address to the Ephesian elders, he said, "After my departure fierce wolves will come in among you, not sparing the flock" (Acts 20:29). He was talking about false teachers. And John warned that the spirit of antichrist was already loose in the churches. It was this that was behind some church members' denial of a real incarnation (1 John 2:22; 4:3).

This process, and this kind of attack, continued unabated. But it reached a particularly critical point in the teaching of Arius, a presbyter in Alexandria, early in the fourth century. His teaching itself was not particularly novel or particularly brilliant, but Arius had followers, and that was the problem. We might think of him as a forerunner of the Jehovah's Witnesses.

His argument was that Christ was not the eternal second person of the Godhead. Rather, he was created at some point in time prior to the creation. He was made and not begotten.[9]

On the face of it, this was an attack on the divinity of Christ and therefore on the Trinity as well. Arius, though, had his subtleties. In his view, there could be different degrees of divinity, rather like the layers of a cake. So one could think of Christ as being divine power, God's intermediary to the world, but this power was something other than and less than the Father's. This was, in all likelihood, a pagan way of thinking that had entered Arius's mind. At the very least, he was rationalistic. He exploited the difference between the Father who, in his essence, is completely changeless and the Son who, as he grew and developed, did change. The Son was different from the Father and could not have been coeternal. The Son had to have been created at some moment prior to the creation of the world.

As this teaching began to gather momentum, making alliances with the spirit of paganism as well as with Jews hostile to the Christian faith, the church found itself confronted by a challenge that, once again, was threatening its very life. It had survived the external challenge of persecution led by the Roman emperors, though at great personal cost, but now it was facing an even more difficult challenge, one that was internal. It was the challenge posed by false teachers.

All the church's leaders were called together in a council to address this situation, much like the apostles and elders had gathered together early on at Jerusalem (Acts 15:1–35). But this subsequent gathering was far larger than that of the apostles, and it was to produce a decisive creed in the year 325. The Nicene Creed, which the council wrote, has been embraced, and is used today, in all the main branches of Christianity: Roman Catholicism, Eastern Orthodoxy, and Protestantism.

Most immediately, it had to address the nature of Christ's divinity, since this was where the frontal assault lay. But implicit in the attack was a rejection of the Trinity as well. The Creed, as a result, devoted most of its attention to the person of Christ. Indeed, the third member of the Godhead, the Holy Spirit, was almost passed over in silence. All the Council said was that it believed "in the Holy Spirit." But this deficiency was addressed later, when his full divinity was explicitly asserted after it had been denied much as Christ's had been.

With respect to Christ, the Council declared that "the Son is from the substance of the Father." This is curious language for us today. Did the Council mean that Christ is the same stuff as the Father? The problem that the Nicene fathers had was that whatever biblical language they tried to use to express the thought that the Son is divine in the same sense as is the Father, the Arians found a way to slide by it or to twist it. They would agree to such language, provided they could interpret it in their own way. So it was that the Nicene fathers ended up with an extrabiblical word, *homoousios*, to express their conviction. This expressed the truth that the Father and the Son share the same divine being. They are God in exactly the same way. And the Nicene framers then reinforced this thought with the phrases "God from God, light from light, true God from true God."

This central affirmation was then bolstered by a related thought. It was that the Son is "begotten, not made." This language may not communicate as clearly today as it once did, when these phrases carried a great deal of weight. The difference between begetting and creating is that in the one, the same thing comes forth, but in the other it does not. Birds, we might say, beget birds. What begets and what is begotten are alike. But this is different from the work of creating. Sculptors make statues that are different from the people whom they represent. And even when the statue is an exact replica of a person, no one confuses the statue with the person whose image it is or thinks that they are the same thing. Christ was begotten, not created. So, if like begets like, then Christ's divinity is identical with the Father's divinity.

Sometime after this conflict, in the fifth century, after the church had been rescued from the hands of the Arians, a creed emerged which summed up its consensus. It was known as the Athanasian Creed. It declared in part that the universal faith in the churches was:

That we worship one God in Trinity, and Trinity in Unity; neither confounding the Persons, nor dividing the Substance; for there is one Person of the Father, another of the Son, and another of the Holy Ghost. But the Godhead of the Father, of the Son, and of the Holy Ghost is all one. . . . So the Father is God, the Son is God, and the Holy Spirit is God. And yet there are not three Gods but one God. The Godhead of the Father, and of the Son, and of the Holy Ghost is all one, the Glory equal, the Majesty coeternal. . . . And in this Trinity none is afore or after the other; none is greater or less than the other, but the whole three Persons are coeternal together and coequal. . . . The Unity in Trinity and the Trinity in Unity is to be worshipped.

By our standards today, this may seem a bit complex, and yet the ideas are not that difficult. Indeed, they are central to the Christian faith.

We in the West are not seduced today by the thought of multiple deities, or of creations before creation, or of a Son who is divine but not in the same sense as the Father. Aside from the Jehovah's Witnesses, this kind of speculation has disappeared. People either believe in the divinity of Christ or they do not.

What we are susceptible to is a little different. It is the allure of modalism, which is the other heresy being addressed in this creed. It is the habit of speaking of the Trinity as simply the three ways in which God presents himself to us. It is as though he simply puts on temporary, impermanent masks. The presumption is that these are just the three ways in which he has revealed himself. On this view, the Father, the Son, and the Holy Spirit are not three persons who are eternal and eternally distinct from one another; rather, they are three phases of, or three "looks" to, the same God.

Many in our churches today are unknowing modalists. If they use Trinitarian language at all, it is largely meaningless. It is simply what they have heard. What they believe in is God. Sometimes they speak of him as Father, sometimes as Son, and sometimes as Holy Spirit. These are but different names for the same thing. And this confusion carries over into some of the prayers we hear in church, where it seems to be a matter of indifference whether it was the Father who went to the Cross or the Son, whether we approach the Father through the Son or through the Spirit, and whether Father and Son become distant, even irrelevant, if we have the Spirit.

This confusion may seem innocent enough. Behind it, it is true, is no ill intent. However, our fumbling inability to grasp the Trinity, to articulate it clearly, to affirm the biblical truths on which it is founded, only portends greater confusion down the road. This is so because it shows how far we have drifted from the teaching of Scripture, or how loosely we treat it, how tolerant we are of personal spiritualities and ways of expressing ourselves. It is this drifting from our biblical moorings that portends an unhappy future. We cannot dispense with the Trinity, as God has revealed himself to be, without losing the Christian faith as God has established it.

CONNECTIONS TO PRACTICE

Because this doctrine of God's triunity is interwoven throughout the whole fabric of the Christian faith—or, should we say that the Christian faith arises out of the Trinity and therefore is always Trinitarian in its shape?—it provides the grounding for much of our practice. At least, it should. Here I can only illustrate this with respect to two matters: evangelism and prayer. The principles, though, apply across a much broader swath of the Christian life.

The Gospel

The Trinitarian connections to the gospel are nowhere more profoundly developed than in Ephesians 1:1–14. There the gospel is related specifically to the three members of the Godhead. Salvation originates in the electing work of the Father. Before "the foundation of the world," he "chose us" (1:4). This salvation is carried through and achieved by the Son, in whom we have "redemption through his blood" (1:7). And once we have believed the gospel, by the internal, illuminating work of the Spirit, we have been "sealed with the promised Holy Spirit" (1:13). Here it is: the work of Father, Son, and Holy Spirit.

There is, though, much more to the passage than this. If the Father is the author of election, then the Son is its means, and the Spirit is its agent. In this we see the will of God being realized (1:5, 9), for he is the one who "works all things according to the counsel of his will" (1:11). However, the Father's saving will is not an abstract decree that is simply announced. Rather, Paul states repeatedly that it is worked out *through* Christ. The truth is that we cannot know this will except as we know it in and through Christ (1:9). It is only expressed in Christ, and we must be *in him* in order to know the Father's will. We are blessed only in Christ (1:3, 6). Only in him have we been chosen (1:4, 11), redeemed (1:7), and brought to a place of hope (1:12). We are able to see that he has now begun to exercise his sovereignty in a new way, for, following the resurrection, he is far above all earthly powers (1:21). It is on him that our love, faith, and hope are now centered.

And yet we would see none of this if the Holy Spirit had not opened our eyes, even as he did Lydia's (Acts 16:14), to pay attention to the truth declared in God's Word, to believe it and embrace it. It is, in fact, the Holy Spirit who links the past of our election by the Father (1:4–5) to the present of our experience of Christ's work at the cross in our stead (1:7), and that to the future of "our inheritance" in the joy and presence of God (1:14). Thus it is that Father, Son, and Holy Spirit are united in their common work of redeeming lost sinners and bringing them to glory.

The gospel, then, is not simply about finding hope or meaning, or making a commitment, or being born again. It is about all of those things because it is first and foremost about being reconciled to the Father, from whom we have been alienated, by the work of Christ on the cross, in order that we might be forgiven and know him. This begins, not in our choices, but in the Father's. Without the Father's electing work, none would be saved, whereas now, because of it, some are being saved. And without the illuminating work of the Spirit and his application of the redemption that Christ has won for us, we would not see and would not want the very thing of which we stand most in need. The Father's election, the Son's sacrifice for us and in our place, and the Spirit's application of this work, all remind us that we bring nothing to our salvation except the sin from which we need to be redeemed. God—Father, Son, and Holy Spirit—has done it all, and he has done it from first to last. When we think about the gospel, these are the connections that should come immediately to our minds. And if what comes to mind has lost some of these connections, then to that extent our understanding of the gospel has become skewed.

When we see the lengths to which God's grace has gone, the depth of love that God has shown us in the Son, are we not amazed that all of this sometimes has little effect on us? Too often in the church, who God is and what he has done do not much determine who we are and what we do. The churches are full of people who live little differently from how they did before they "decided for Christ." In 2006, George Barna found that only 15 percent of "born-again" Christians said that God was their first priority in life. This is a scandal. It is important for us to remind ourselves that the purpose of God's election is that "we should be holy and blameless before him" (Eph. 1:4). In the absence of this kind of upright character—this God-centeredness that should be the outcome of the grace that has reached us in Christ—the Christian faith is mightily discredited.

Why are there so many who can assent to the essentials of the Christian faith and yet live as if they had never heard the gospel? Undoubtedly there are many reasons. But this much can said with certainty. Our entire culture—consumer driven, entertainment oriented, technologically alive—has the effect of making people radically autonomous. The reasons for this, and the mechanisms by which it works, are complex, but the effects are to be seen everywhere in the churches today. If God and orthodoxy are affirmed, the rest of life is nevertheless seen from the vantage point of the autonomous self, the person to whom nothing is real that is not felt and about which personal choices have been made. Reality becomes what we say it is, what we choose it to be—and what we want to say it is has to do with the here and now, with buying and selling, with having and enjoying, with being free from all inconveniences. In this self-made environment, this self-centered psychology, God becomes insignificant, no matter how orthodox we profess ourselves to be. There are many churches that have simply rolled over and capitulated to this modern mood, to this consumer mentality. They are found across the entire theological spectrum, from Arminian to Reformed.

What follows from all of this is that Christ disappears and the Christian faith becomes indistinguishable from our all-pervasive consumer culture. The gospel is reduced to little more than a product of self-help therapy, and Christianity becomes a lifestyle that is no more true than any other lifestyle, no more compelling—just something that we put on at our convenience.

Clearly, knowing the biblical doctrine of the Trinity and how Father, Son, and Spirit have worked out their divine mission through the gospel is not the only answer. This knowledge needs to be coupled with an acute understanding of what our culture is like and how it intrudes into the way we see the world, ourselves, and, most importantly, God. Without this discernment, the culture will take our gospel captive, and God will disappear from our view. Without this understanding of what the gospel is and how it expresses the will and work of Father, Son, and Holy Spirit, we have no alternative to the reality that our consumer culture is spinning in place of God. Today we urgently need a renewal in both this orthodoxy and this cultural discernment.

Prayer

The Holy Spirit gives us both the status and the experience of being children of our heavenly Father. The opening section in Ephesians addresses our status in Christ. Now we need to think about our experience of that status. Specifically, it is the connection with prayer that is in view here. And prayer, like the gospel, is shaped by the reality of God as triune.

We pray to the Father, through Christ our mediator, by the Holy Spirit. That is the basic New Testament pattern.

And yet this is no mere rote performance. In two of the remarkable passages we have already noted, Paul deepens the meaning of prayer in a way that we do not want to miss.

In both of these passages, Paul speaks of our knowing that we are God's children because of the Spirit's work. In Galatians 4:6, the "Spirit of his Son" is sent into our hearts to cry "Abba! Father!" In Romans 8:16–17, we learn that the Spirit bears witness with our spirits, as a result of which we cry, "Abba! Father!"

Were these two passages to stand by themselves, we might wonder what this untranslated word, "Abba," really means. What should we make of it? It does, however, have a context in the biblical narrative. It is the garden of Gethsemane. Jesus was in deep anguish. He was being tested to the limit, and turned to his Father in prayer. "Abba, Father," he said, "all things are possible for you. Remove this cup from me. Yet not what I will, but what you will" (Mark 14:36).

It is Jesus' own language from this moment of deep communion with his Father that is now put into the souls of believers. The Holy Spirit, who has been "sent" into our hearts, who is bearing witness with our spirits, himself speaks this cry in our inner being as he points us to the Father.

From these words in Paul's letters, we should draw at least two conclusions. First, it is God's intent that we be *assured* of our status as his children. This is something we are to experience in our innermost self. Perhaps the Holy Spirit's assurance comes at different times and in different ways. He knows when we are most perplexed, weighed down with suffering, and anxious to find the guidance of God amidst our circumstances. And he knows when, in times of waywardness, we are not susceptible to such assurance and are not wanting or seeking it. But regardless of the circumstances of our lives, Christ, who is our shepherd, knows how to lead us and where to lead us. To the Holy Spirit has been given this work of assuring us that this is so. Thus it is that we lift our heads with confidence as we reach up in prayer to our heavenly Father. We are his beloved children!

Second, these words from Paul assure us, not only that we will have an audience with our Father, but that we are encouraged to come into his presence. For what earthly father who is worthy of the name *father* is disinterested in his children, unwilling to hear them, or ready to abandon them? If our earthly fathers know how to give us good things, Jesus said, so much more does our heavenly Father know how to do so. And it is this thought that is conveyed by the word *Abba*. It should probably be translated "dearest Father." It is the address of affection, and it conveys the tone of intimacy, even as we see this modeled in the relationship between the Son and the Father.

That being so, how often we should be in our Father's presence in prayer! We should run to him, as children do to their earthly parents, to give thanks for our joys, to unburden ourselves of our sorrows before him, to seek his kingdom, and to give ourselves to his service.

There is so much more than we now know about God's glorious being and his triune nature. We stand at the edge of a vast ocean and see just its shoreline. We cannot see beyond the horizon, though we can be entirely confident that what we cannot know about God is fully consistent with what we do know because of his self-revelation to us. Although there is so much more, we cannot allow ourselves to have any less than what God has given us. Without the triune God, one being in three persons, we do not have the biblical God and we do not have the Christian faith. Taking hold of what

God has given us, treasuring it, living it, and proclaiming it is now our task during this, our short, earthly life and pilgrimage. "For from him and through him and to him are all things. To him be glory forever. Amen" (Rom. 11:36).

Glory be to the Father, and to the Son, and to the Holy Ghost: As it was in the beginning, is now and ever shall be, world without end. Amen.

NOTES

1   Benjamin B. Warfield, *Biblical and Theological Studies*, ed. Samuel G. Craig (Philadelphia: Presbyterian and Reformed, 1952), 35.

2   John Hick, *God Has Many Names* (Philadelphia: Westminster, 1982), 107–9. Hick at times retains the language of the Trinity, but, for example, he sees Christ as being the unknown presence in the other religions and regards these religions as responses to the universal Spirit. See his *A Christian Theology of Religions: The Rainbow of Faiths* (Louisville: Westminster John Knox, 1995).

3   In the section that follows, I am summarizing what I first wrote in *The Person of Christ: A Biblical and Historical Analysis of the Incarnation* (Wheaton, IL: Crossway Books, 1984) and then extended in *Above All Earthly Pow'rs: Christ in a Postmodern World* (Grand Rapids: Eerdmans, 2005).

4   God is occasionally spoken of as being the Father of all, but, in these cases, only in the sense that he is the Creator of all. See Acts 17:28–29; Eph. 3:14ff.; Heb. 12:9; James 1:17. Although God is the Father of all in this sense, sinners refuse to come to terms with this fact and reject the implications of this knowledge (Rom. 1:18–21).

5   J. I. Packer, *Knowing God* (Downers Grove, IL: InterVarsity Press, 1973), 201.

6   The attempt to identify God as feminine, which has been pursued by a number of feminist writers, invariably leads into pantheism. See Elizabeth Achtemeier, *Nature, God and Pulpit* (Grand Rapids: Eerdmans, 1992), 20–39.

7 In the following section on the person and work of the Holy Spirit, I show my indebtedness to a consultation on this subject organized by the Lausanne Committee on World Evangelization, which I subsequently wrote up as *God the Evangelist: How the Holy Spirit Works to Bring Men and Women to Faith* (Grand Rapids: Eerdmans, 1987).

8 Charles Hodge, *Systematic Theology* (3 vols.; repr., Grand Rapids: Eerdmans, 1952), 1:444.

9 The framers of the Nicene Creed summarized Arius's teaching in a brief concluding section. This was included in the Creed but is typically omitted today. It states: "But as for those who say, There was a time when he was not, and, before being born he was not, and that he came into existence out of nothing, or who assert that the Son of God is of a different hypostasis or substance, or is created, or is subject to alteration or change—these the Catholic Church anathematizes."

MORE ABOUT THE TRINITY FROM P&R PUBLISHING

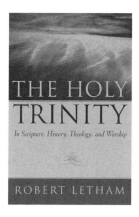

Robert Letham offers a well-researched volume about "the One who is utterly transcendent and incomprehensible." After examining the doctrine's biblical foundations, he traces its historical development through the twentieth century and engages four critical issues: the Trinity and (1) the incarnation, (2) worship and prayer, (3) creation and missions, and (4) persons.

"In this outstanding work, Letham points us back to God in all the mystery and glory of his triune being. With his keen theological acumen, Letham has given us a tour de force of Reformed theology."
—**Sinclair B. Ferguson**, senior minister, First Presbyterian Church, Columbia, South Carolina

"Solid and judicious, comprehensive and thorough, abreast of past wisdom and present-day debate, and doxological in tone throughout, this is far and away the best big textbook on the Trinity that you can find, and it will surely remain so for many years to come."
—**J. I. Packer**, professor of theology, Regent College, Vancouver, British Columbia

TRUTH FOR LIFE®

Truth For Life is the Bible-teaching ministry of Alistair Begg. Our mission is to teach the Bible with clarity and relevance so that unbelievers will be converted, believers will be established, and local churches will be strengthened.

Since 1995, Truth For Life has accomplished its mission on the radio, online, and in print. Every day we release a new Bible-teaching message on over 1,600 radio outlets around the world and through our website and daily podcast.

A large content archive is available on our website, where listeners can download free messages or purchase CDs and DVDs of Alistair Begg's sermons. Printed publications, authored by Alistair Begg, address a variety of life's challenges, yet always point back to the authority and truth of God's Word.

Truth For Life also connects with listeners at live ministry events and conferences across the U.S. and Canada in cities where the radio program is heard.

CONTACT TRUTH FOR LIFE

In the U.S.:
P.O. Box 398000, Cleveland, OH 44139
www.truthforlife.org · letters@truthforlife.org
1-888-588-7884

In Canada:
P.O. Box 132, Maple Ridge, BC V2X 7E9
www.truthforlife.ca · letters@truthforlife.ca
1-877-518-7884

And also at:
www.facebook.com/truthforlife
www.twitter.com/truthforlife